PRESS FOR ACTION

POETRY

Mike Gould
Alison Tunstall

SERIES EDITORS

David Orme
James Sale

Many of the poems in this book are examples of children's own work. They are the result of working in Denbigh High School classes with the poetry of Michael Rosen, Tom Leonard, Phillip Paddon and Carl Sandburg. The authors would like to acknowledge their debt to them.

Thanks also to *The Radio Times*, to BBC Radio 4, Bristol, Susan Roberts in particular, to the *Blue Peter* programme and to the *Schools' Poetry Association* for their co-operation.

ISBN 1 85276075 3
First published 1990 by Folens Limited, Albert House, Apex Business Centre, Boscombe Road, Dunstable LU5 4RL

Covers by Abacus Publicity Ltd.
Illustrations by Linda Robson

Printed in Great Britain by Kenley Press, Dunstable.

CONTENTS

SYMBOLS/TEACHER RESOURCE INDICATORS

 Early Voices Section

 Early Voices Radio Module

 Eye Lines Section

 Eye Lines TV Module

 World View Section

 World View Film Module

 Mind Words Section

 Mind Words Press Module

 Cassette tape-recorder can be used

 Video camera can be used

 Record Box for self-evaluation/further work

INTRODUCTION

   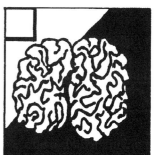

This is a new kind of poetry book. It attempts to combine a practical approach to poetry analysis and writing with a general examination of basic media.

It takes the pupil on a journey of sorts, if the teacher wishes to follow the whole book as a course. However our aim is to provide the non-specialist English teacher, as well as the specialist, with the opportunity to dip into whatever section they feel necessary. Most of the units stand up on their own, but the sub-sections on radio, TV, film and the press, lend themselves more easily to a modular, course-work approach. We also aim to cover a wide variety of the areas demanded by the National Curriculum and to that end do not steer away from work on the acquisition of language skills.

Although the book has a strong media input, it is always the poetry that is the greatest concern....the media service the poetry and not visa versa. To this end, the overall concept that informs the book is the notion of the primary senses of **SOUND** and **SIGHT** followed by **MIND.** The media are merely a convenient way of focussing on these areas.

The book is practical. It is our intention that pupils should enjoy the work and where possible produce something. The idea behind the record box is that all pupils should be constantly evaluating what they have done and looking forward to further work.

As far as the poetry itself, we have included children's own writing, either by pupils we know, or from established sources such as the major national poetry competitions. Furthermore, we have attempted to provide lesser known poets, like Habib Jalib, with a platform for their poems; too many poets are over anthologised. Shakespeare is our major exception!

Built into the structure are clear symbols for the teacher and pupil alike to guide them in their study, but it must be made clear that none of the units are disbarred if one does not have access to the equipment suggested.

Finally, this is not a comprehensive text that deals with every single area and issue connected with poetry; it is a broad, dynamic way-in for pupils to ensure that the love of poetry many develop in their younger years is maintained throughout their school life .... and beyond.

Mike Gould and Alison Tunstall.

TEACHERS' NOTES

EARLY VOICES

This section deals with **SOUND** in its most general sense. It aims to introduce the pupil to an awareness of how words sound, how sounds are used, how poems should be performed....and so on. Sound is the primary sense that precedes sight, hence the order in this book. However, sound cannot exist outside content and form, so there is a necessary network of ideas that come together in this section. A module on radio is included as a way of combining appreciation of this aural medium with some creative/critical work on aspects of poetry.

7. **New Faces:** Work on dialogue, punctuation, performance, creation of own oral poems.
8. **Sounds Good:** Made-up words (neologisms), sound words.
9. **Sounds Better:** Improving performance of poems, key words, evaluation.
10. **Sound Snaps:** Sounds of words, syllables.
11. **Snapshots:** Patterns, syllables, haiku.
12. **Rhyme Tree:** Variety of rhyme, memorising poems, cinquain.

RADIO.

13. **Radio Requests:** *Poetry Please* radio research, analysis of title, content and form.
14. **Final Countdown:** *Poetry Please 2*, cinquain, finishing poems, letter writing, cloze.
15. **Broadcast Time:** Radio show performance, research, discursive writing.
16. **Codewords:** Similes, extract from *Macbeth,* essay writing, riddles.
17. **Poetic Messages:** Abbreviations, speech on important issues, message poems.

EYE LINES

This section covers various areas of poetry taking the visual aspect, as a focus. The aim of these sheets is to take the pupil through the various stages of writing their own poems examining subjects and forms in more detail than they might have done previously. Pupils are also asked to appreciate/criticise poetry and to discriminate between good and bad. A sub-section is based around the television/news theme, a natural development from more oral/aural concerns of the previous section.

18. **Studio Speak:** Script-writing and presentation, conversation poems.
19. **Conversation:** Writing conversation poems and presenting, script writing.
20. **DIY Ideas:** Poetry Competition, emotions vs. things, brainstorming, prose descriptions.
21. **Formations:** Forms of poetry, cloze.
22. **Pen to Paper:** Final stages of writing, words as building bricks, rules, drafting, analysis.

TV.

23. **You the Judge:** Poetry competition, appreciation, criticism, class decisions.
24. **Newspeak:** Creating news programmes, sequencing, recruiting a team and report poems.
25. **Transmission Time:** Rehearsal, performance, evaluation, other poetry.
26. **Talk Right:** News poem, Standard English, accents, own accent poems, stereotypes.

TEACHERS' NOTES

WORLD VIEW

This section looks at the influence of time and culture on language generally and poetry specifically. A wide-range of diferent poets from different nationalities are examined and there is a concentrated study of Shakespeare and his time in the film section; Shakespeare should be made available to children alongside contemporary poets. This section attempts to bring them together.

27. **Time Travel:** Different languages, Old English poetry, translation, continuation of poems.
28. **Time Travel 2:** Chaucer, translation work, Shakespeare, metaphors.
29. **Word Invaders:** Influence on English language, crossword, American rap.
30. **Culture Talk:** Place as an influence, link-ups.
31. **People Portraits:** Stereotypes.
32. **Angry Voices:** Emotional Poetry, group poems.

FILM.

33. **Document Decision:** Fact-finding on Shakespeare, biographical poem, locations.
34. **Superb Sonnets:** Structure of Sonnets, rhyming couplets, story-board.
35. **Discovered!:** Writing own sonnet, vocabulary, presenting.

MIND WORDS

This section deals with some of the more complex ideas behind poetry, concentrating on some important, as well as frivolous issues, for example, relationships. It encourages pupils to 'interrogate' poems, but in a sub-section on the press returns to a practically-based approach to poetry.

36. **Cover-up :** Anthologies, theme-work, verbs.
37. **Love Story :** Relationships, pop-poetry, happy/sad endings, extended metaphors.
38. **Hidden Talents :** Analysis/interrogation of poems, atmosphere.
39. **Mind Words :** Choosing vocabulary carefully, verbs as spells.

PRESS.

40. **Press for Action :** Selecting articles for a magazine, epitaphs.
41. **Front Page :** Poetry articles, re-writing with a message, bias, research into Betjeman, cloze.
42. **Poetic Power :** Pakistani Poetry, poetry with a message, bias, research.
43. **Visions :** Portrayal of evil, Milton and song lyrics, personal belief, paradox.
44. **Poetry Product :** Pupil poetry magazine how to go about it, stage by stage.

he and she

she: it's the same thing
he: no it is not
she: yes it is
he: let's not go through all that again
she: right
he: why do you always have the last word
she : you have it
he: thank you

(pause)

she: don't mention it
he: why can't you shut up
she: why can't *you* shut up
he: shut up
she: you shut up

(Both together)

he: shut up
she: shut up

R.D. Laing

When you make up a poem you speak to someone; the reader or the person listening. The poem above may help you think about *how* to read poems aloud.

● Look at the pictures of "he" and "she". Discuss with a friend what you think the boy and girl are like. Are they quiet? Shy? Angry? What do you think?

● How would they speak in this poem? Angrily? Nervously? What is the reason behind this argument?

● Put in any question marks and exclamation marks that may be missing. Do they help you to understand how they are speaking?

● **NOW** in pairs perform the poem. Read it with real feeling, as if you were the boy and girl in the pictures.

DIALOGUE.
● What you have just read is a dialogue (or conversation). Write your own dialogue poem.
Choose one of the scenes below:
An argument in a shoe shop.
Trying to get more pocket money.
A chat with a friend about a great film.

● What do you think is the most difficult thing about reading aloud?
● Find out where the word DIALOGUE comes from.
● What is a DIALECT?

This page may be photocopied for classroom use only.

SOUNDS GOOD

Sometimes poets give us clues to tell us how to read poems. Often words themselves describe sounds or actions.

Pitter

Patter

Boiling

Say these words like the things they describe. eg. hissssssssssss....

Splooching along in the thick heavy soil
Spludgily, ploopily, splush
Two heavy feet sunk in red gooey ****
Gloopoly, malumpomy, bloop
Plogolysplodgoly say my ****
Flushopy, splushopy, glop
Quickly jump on to solid earth
Crunchingly, galumphingly, hard
But, ugh, I'm up to my knees again
Spludgily, ploopily, splush...

Permindar Sethi

● Try to work out which two words are missing from Permindar's poem. They give away the title of the poem.

● Which of the words in the poem are "made up"? Make a list. If you are not sure, look them up in a dictionary.

● The words the poet chose were just right for describing the sounds of the poem. Make a list of *made up* words (also known as *neologisms*) to go with the three pictures below.

A STREAM	THUNDER AND LIGHTNING	AN EARTHQUAKE

REAL SOUND WORDS.
● Supply the most appropriate sound words for:
bacon frying........sizzle...............
a high-pitched laugh........................
saucepans falling............................
newspapers folding........................
a door shutting...............................

● What was your favourite neologism? Can you say why?
● What does the prefix "NEO" mean in front of a word?

SOUNDS BETTER

A poetry evening is to be held at your school. You have been chosen to read the poem below, BUT you've never read a poem aloud in front of lots of people before. Read the poem below carefully, then consider the tasks that follow.

Baby Breakfast.

Squidge
My food in my fist
Throw
It at the wall
Rub
It in my hair
Soak
It in my milk
Squeeze the dirt out
Stuff
It in my mouth
Splurt
It across the room
Dig
It out of my bib
Catapult
It to Mummy
Aim
It at Daddy
Mmmm
Finished.

Julie Marsden (15)

Here is a list of things to think about when reading aloud. Put them in order of importance (eg if you think (c) *smiling* is the most important, then put **1** next to it).

- *a) keeping the same look on your face*
- *b) not making mistakes*
- *c) smiling*
- *d) changing the sound of your voice*
- *e) reading slowly*
- *f) looking at the audience*
- *g) making important words stand out.*

● Which are the key words in the poem you think should stand out when you read? Underline them.

● Compare your list with a friend. Did you agree?

● Practise reading the poem in a group. Give marks out of 10 for the best performance.

● Write your own poem called MEALTIME. It should include plenty of carefully chosen sound words.

● Hold a WORST reading competition in your class in which you deliberately do badly! What would be the worst things to do? Whisper? Stand on your head?

● There is a special word we use to describe words that SOUND like the things that are talked about. Is it....
a) CORNUCOPIA
b) ONOMATOPOEIA
c) MOZZARELLA?

SOUND SNAPS

Choosing words carefully in poetry is particularly important because you are rarely writing in full sentences. Sometimes one or two words on a line will say all you want. Writing about animals always gives good opportunities for colourful descriptions, but finding the right word isn't always as easy.

● Put the words below under their correct animal headings.

> sliding   oozing   flit   swift
> clumsily   bellowing   dart
> drip   gigantic   trundling
> dip   rumbling   spiral
> flick   sleek   dive
> unwinding   crashing   quick

Elephant walking.	Otter diving.	Snake climbing.

Here are two fairly obvious connections: an elephant *bellowing* and *quick* as an otter. In fact the words fit the sound/action of the animals. *Bellowing* is a long, round word....good for an elephant, and *quick* is short and sharp, like an otter. In fact *QUICK* has one syllable. *BELLOWING* has three. Most of your words in the *ELEPHANT* list will sounder longer than in the otter list.

WHAT IS A SYLLABLE?
A syllable is the sound-part of a word. For example....

1	2	3
bel	low	ing
quick		

HOW MANY SYLLABLES IN YOUR NAME?
Chris - to - pher has three.

● Write your own description in prose or verse of either a tortoise (use long, slow words and vowel sounds) or of a mouse (using quick, short, sharp words and vowel sounds).
● Brainstorm words first and put them into a list.
● Test them out by speaking the words appropriately to a partner so he or she can guess what kind of movement or action you are describing.

SNAPSHOTS

Many different poems use a particular number of syllables to achieve a particular effect. The most famous form is perhaps the **HAIKU** which is a Japanese form of poetry. To write a haiku you must use only *seventeen syllables in three lines* and these must be arranged in a particular pattern. The first line should have only five syllables, the second seven syllables and the third five syllables again. Each word must be chosen very carefully in order to surprise the reader with your view of something or somebody. A haiku lets you capture a snapshot of life in just three lines.

Silently stalking
Imagined prey, my small cat,
Brave, twitches in sleep.

Intent, the bee hums.
Impossible striped barrel
Floats on powder wings.

The dead pond buzzes.
Quick, with green and sudden hop
A fat frog plops in.

Gasping, the trout leaps!
Merging circles below him,
Whirling sky above.

● Here are some words from a haiku jumbled up. See if you can fit them into the form.

**June   cuckoo's   devoured   fruit   the   be   sweetly   trees   in
the   note   to   hangs   still**

● We said Haiku were snapshots. Well, write your own haiku to go with this picture, or use a picture of your own.

● What are the advantages and disadvantages of writing haiku?
● Write a haiku for each month of the year as a group and illustrate the sequence. Find out what a sequence of haiku is called.

RHYME TREE

Below is a "rhyme tree". At the end of its branches it has small sections from poems containing different types of rhyme. What do you think rhyme is? If you're not sure, finish this well known rhyme....

Humpty-dumpty sat on the wall,
Humpty-dumpty had a great ****

● Which of these poems on the tree are perfect rhymes?

Dim pale-eyed fishes near
Gaze at the gilded year.

Rat-tat it went...
"That hat, I know it"

A blue bottle perched on a piece of sardine
What's the horriblest thing that you've ever seen?

I could not move,
Because of love

For of my glee might many men have laughed.
And of my weeping something had been left.

● Try to say what the rhyme is in each case, and how it is different from another pair of lines on the tree. Rhyme is important for many reasons in poetry. Try this simple test. Read both the poems below twice each, cover the page, and then try to say them out loud.

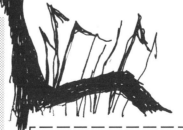

"You are old, Father William," the young man said,
"And your hair has become very white;
And yet you incessantly stand on your head -
Do you think, at your age, it is right?"

Listen,
A whistle blows,
A black hole fills with smoke.
The child awaits red faced, his train
Has gone.

● Which was the easiest? Probably, the first. Why do you think that was? Lewis Carroll`s poem uses simple end-rhymes *(white\right)* which also seem to fit a funny poem. Can you think of any other funny poems? Do they have these type of rhymes?

● REMEMBER! You don't have to use end-rhymes in all your poems. As you have seen there are many more types available. In fact, why use rhymes at all? Well, sometimes they fit the subject...story poems, funny poems etc.

● Try finding words that end-rhyme with:*attic....kettle....monastery....kitchen ....silver....car....latest....flute....cod*
● Write an eight line rhyme about yourself.
● What kinds of rhymes and rhyme schemes have you found out about?

RADIO REQUESTS

POETRY PLEASE

11.40am
Poetry Please!
with **Simon Rae**.
Readers DIANA BISHOP
and JOHN MATSHIKIZA.
Guest **Fred D'Aguiar**
Producer SUSAN ROBER?
BBC Bristol. Stereo

12.00 You and Yours
Presenter **John Waite**
Editor KEN VASS

Radio 4 has a programme called *Poetry Please*. People request their favourite poems by letter. YOU have just been appointed presenter of the programme. Unfortunately, after a recent fire in the studio, the requests, the poems, and their titles, have been mixed up! Here are the fragments. Look at them carefully.

I used to work at nights. All my family were in bed...and there was poor me, out in my delivery van, driving through the countryside in the dark...

Like the ocean
No one with her
She walks alone
Remembering once
The love she had

LONELINESS

She was lovely, she was, with her perfect round face, so calm and peaceful... that's why I chose this poem.

The sea
Was grey and cold

A black and furry shiny ball
Upon the sheets so white
You don't mind rain
You don't mind squalls

MOON

BEACH MEMORIES

It reminds me of when I lived in Brighton. I was an old single man then.

I always think of my gran when I hear this poem. I felt so sorry for her after Grandad died. All she had was....

CAT SLEEPING

White and round
Without a sound
I creep around
I am still...

- You have five minutes to match all three (title, poem and letter) before the producer gets back.....Off you go! Think carefully about what the poems/letters are about; there are connections.
- Write down your reasons for matching them up.
- Did your class-mates have the same results as you?
- Discuss any differences of opinion with them.

RECORD BOX

- Look at the *Radio Times*. How many programmes are about poetry or poets? Make a list of their titles.
- Listen to one and write a brief summary saying what it is about.

POETRY PLEASE (2)

Having sorted out the poems, titles and letters, there is another problem. You can't find the rest of the original poems, even though you now have the titles. However, your producer tells you to go ahead anyway. So, what are you going to do?

CLUES
● You decide to complete the poems yourself, using the clues below that you have been able to find out. The poem about the sea is a part of a CINQUAIN. It should have five lines of 2,4,6,8,2 syllables. Here is an example of a cinquain.

Pie-face
I knew
A round-faced boy.
He ate, and ate, so many pies,
He died full-up, but I was left
Empty.

● The poem, *White and round* has three verses each with the same number of lines.
● *Like the ocean* has one verse of fifteen lines. It doesn't rhyme.
● *A black and furry shiny ball*...NO CLUES with this one!

● Next get into groups of three/four. Discuss your efforts. Your boss suggests you broadcast your ideas. Perhaps the audience won't mind the changes. However, you need to decide in your group which poems will be the ones read. Fill these roles as well:
a) presenter
b) reader 1
c) reader 2
d) producer (responsible for recording/sound effects/music.....plus final decisions about the choice of poems etc.)

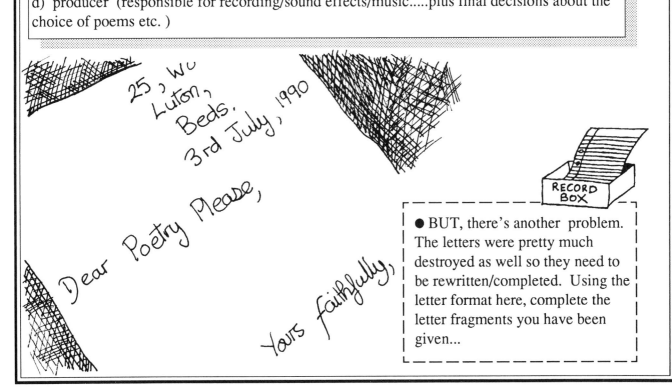

25, Wc
Luton,
Beds.
3rd July, 1990

Dear Poetry Please,

Yours faithfully,

● BUT, there's another problem. The letters were pretty much destroyed as well so they need to be rewritten/completed. Using the letter format here, complete the letter fragments you have been given...

RECORD BOX

BROADCAST TIME

POETRY PLEASE (3)

● Now perform the programme in front of the class. Remember to make it sound like a radio programme. (eg.introduction/music etc.)
● Tape your programme if you wish.
● Create a follow-up programme containing your own favourite poems and why you chose them (a sort of *Desert Island Poems*!)
● Carry out a survey in your class about radio-listening and television-viewing habits.

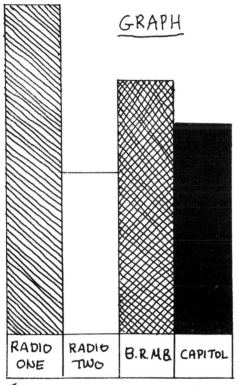

GRAPH

RADIO ONE | RADIO TWO | B.R.M.B. | CAPITOL

FAVOURITE PROGRAMMES.

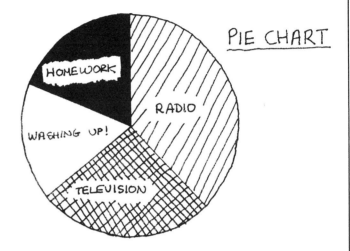

PIE CHART

HOMEWORK
RADIO
WASHING UP!
TELEVISION

1. How often do the people in your class listen to the radio?
2. What station do they normally listen to?
3. What do they like best about it?
4. Do they spend more time watching T.V?
5. How many T.V. programmes about poetry can you find?

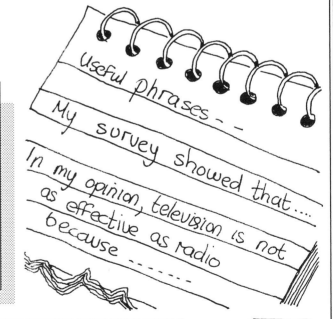

Useful phrases – –
My survey showed that....
In my opinion, television is not as effective as radio because – – – – –

Radio Research
● Radio is a great way to present poetry because it makes you concentrate on the words. Some poeple might say that television is better because you can make videos or films to go with the poems. What do you think?
● You may wish to present your findings in an unusual/visual way. Try making a wall chart with different colours for T.V. hours/radio hours...or for different programmes.

● Write down which you prefer, television or radio.....and why.
● Which do you think is better for presenting poetry?
● Did you find out anything interesting from your survey and charts?

RECORD BOX

CODEWORDS

You are a SPY working for England in a country called Ecossia, where they speak a strange sort of English. You are hiding in a government building when one night you hear the following conversation on your rather old radio. Unluckily, it's rather faint and you only hear snatches...

"My dearest love, Duncan comes here tonight..."

"And when goes....?"

"Tomorrow...."

"O never
Shall sun that morrow see. Your face, my.....
is a book where men
May read strange matters. To beguile the time,
look like the time; bear welcome in your eye,
Your hand, your tongue; look like the innocent flower,
But be the serpent under't. He's that coming
Must be provided for......."

● You suspect something nasty is going to happen. What are these two going to do to Duncan when he comes? You must find out!

● You taped the conversation. What proof is there that danger is lurking for Duncan? Make a list of any words or phrases that suggest this. Look up any words you don't know in the GLOSSARY. (beguile, morrow, serpent)

● You probably wrote down the word 'serpent'. If someone is like a serpent or snake, are they a good or bad person? If you said someone is like a lamb then we'd think of them as being gentle. This is a **SIMILE.**

● Now send your own message back to England, telling the government that some people are planning to murder an important man called Duncan. It'll have to be in code so try to make it sound like the conversation above... eg. *Two greedy lizards are about to eat a small chick.* (It doesn't have to be about animals)

● Make your own secret tape.

● Write a story based around your experiences as a spy in Ecossia. Call it *How I saved Duncan.*

● You need to get to Ecossia. Send a coded message which contains these details.....
Arrive 5.30 in morning by wooden boat. I'll be wearing red gloves, carrying daffodils and walking with a limp.

● Decode this riddle:
A box without hinges, key or lid,golden treasure inside is hid. Make comparisons to help you.

● Find out what famous story by Shakespeare contains the murder of a king called Duncan in it.

This page may be photocopied for classroom use only.

POETIC MESSAGES

The radio has always played an important part in times of war. Many years ago people used to huddle round the old wireless listening for news of battles, bombs, victory or defeat. Imagine hearing the following poem by Peter Porter....or perhaps it's a speech, over the radio....

YOUR ATTENTION PLEASE
The Polar DEW has just warned that
A nuclear rocket strike of
At least one thousand megatons
Has been launched by the enemy
Directly at our major cities
This announcement will take
Two and a quarter minutes to make,
You therefore have a further
Eight and a quarter minutes
To comply with the shelter
Requirements published in the Civil
Defence Code - section Atomic Attack.
A specially shortened Mass
WIll be broadcast at the end
Of this announcement -
Protestant and Jewish services
Will begin simultaneously -
Select your wave length immediately
According to instructions
In the Defence Code. Do not
Take well-loved pets (including birds)
Into your shelter - they will consume
Fresh air. Leave the old and bed-
Ridden, you can do nothing for them.
Remember to press the sealing
Switch when everyone is in
The shelter. Set the radiation
Aerial, turn on the geiger barometer.
Turn off your Television now.
Turn off your radio immediately

The Services end. At the same time
Secure explosion plugs in the ears
Of each member of your family. Take
Down your plasma flasks. Give your children
The pills marked one and two
In the C.D. green container, then put
Them to bed. Do not break
The inside airlock seals until
The radiation All Clear shows
(Watch for the cuckoo in your
perspex panel), or your District
Touring Doctor rings your bell.
If before this, your air becomes
Exhausted or if any of your family
Is critically injured administer
The capsules marked 'Valley Forge'
(Red Pocket in No.1 Survival Kit)
For painless death. (Catholics
Will have been instructed by their priests
What to do in this eventuality)
This announcement is ending - Our President
Has already given orders for
Massive retaliation - it will be
Decisive. Some of us may die
Remember, statistically
It is not likely to be you.
All flags are flying fully dressed
On Government buildings - the sun is shining
Death is the least we have to fear.
We are all in the hands of God,
Whatever happens happens by His Will.
Now go quickly to your shelters.

● This poem is full of instructions, but what do we find out about the poet's feelings?
● Choose two strange instructions in the poem and explain them.
● Imagine you were given five minutes to read a speech or a poem to the whole world about a very important issue. What would you want it to be about?
● Write your poem or speech and perform/ tape it. You need to think carefully about what form would suit your poem best. For an example, would a limerick be a good way of writing about the evil of war?

● "I think the most important thing that needs changing in the world is..............?
● Whose abbreviations? C.N.D. A.L.F. P.L.O.

STUDIO SPEAK

In groups of four perform the following script from an imaginary *Blue Peter* programme and the poem that is included.

Blue Peter Script 12/6/1989
BBC
Mark......and thank you for that interesting story about clothes pegs. Now we have some news of a terrific competition for you to enter.
Caron.....Your school will soon receive details, but, as a clue here we have two young people to perform a poem *'Doors'*.

(Enter pupil 1 and 2 stage right. They sit, facing each other and recite the poem below....TRY RECORDING IT)

DOORS

1. WHEN A DOOR IS WIDE OPEN   IT INVITES YOU
2.   I wonder what's inside
1.   IF A DOOR IS FAST CLOSED
2. but I'm afraid to find out
1.   IT DETERS YOU
2. If I could get through to the other side
1.   SILENT SPIRITS   GLIDE SECRETLY THROUGH
2.   Probably just an empty room
1. CLOSED DOORS   SECRET SPIRIT DOORS
2.   or maybe not
1.   WHEN A DOOR IS FAST CLOSED
2. I want to open it   and to find out for sure
1. IT INVITES YOU TO   OPEN IT
2.   Just a peek   and then I'll know
1. IT DEMANDS YOU OPEN IT   SILENT DOORS
2.   And if there's something special
1.   THEY KNOW MANY SECRETS
2. I promise   I'll not tell a soul
1. BUT THEY WILL NEVER TELL

by **Toby Lurie**.

● Look at the way the poem fits together, and cross out the wrong statement below.

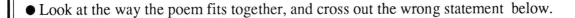

'The lines written by the poet are in capital/small letters'

'The comments by the reader of the poem are in capital/small letters'

● Toby Lurie has created a way of letting you chat with a poem: eg. the original poem says......*WHEN A DOOR IS WIDE OPEN IT INVITES YOU*. The reader wants to know what's in the room so says.....*I wonder what's inside?*

CONVERSATION

● Write your own CONVERSATION poem with this famous and macabre ballad *The Hearse Song*. Your comments can be serious or funny; you can agree or disagree with the poem.

eg. the third line is FOR YOU KNOW SOME DAY   IT'LL GET YOU TOO

You could put   *When? Next Friday?*   *No it won't!*

The old Grey Hearse goes rolling by,
You don't know whether to laugh or cry;
For you know someday it'll get you too,
And the hearse's next load may consist of you.

They'll take you out, and they'll lower you down,
While men with shovels stand all around;
They'll throw in dirt, and they'll throw in rocks,
And they won't give a damn if they break the box.

And your eyes drop out and your teeth fall in,
And the worms crawl over your mouth and chin;
They invite their friends and their friends' friends too
And you look like hell when they're through with you!

● Record this on tape, with as much expression as you can - anger? sadness? humour?

Blue Peter Script..
Mark: ....and we're delighted to be the first TV show to present this new type of poem.
Caron: ....yes, and now we have news of the competition.
Yvette:....All you have to do is write a poem on any subject you like, and send it to the Schools' Poetry Association.
Mark: ....There are some fantastic prizes or the winners. *(Cut to shot of prizes)* So we hope there will be stacks of entries!

● Continue writing this script until the end of the programme.
Remember:
stage directions in brackets,
changes in presenter,
outside interviews/items
the end of the show.
● What would be the three best prizes for the competition?

● What have you learned about how to set out scripts?

DIY IDEAS

Your school receives this letter:

SCHOOLS' POETRY ASSOCIATION

We are looking for the best young poet in Britain today. All you have to do is to send us your entry on any subject.
Prizes
1st...
2nd..
3rd...

What could be better - any subject and prizes! Write in what prizes you would like. But you have to decide what your subject will be and how to write about it. Just think of all the possibilities!

● Here are some subjects:

me	love	books		photos
London	churches	sunrise	you	
sadness	history	pictures		animals
hate	flowers		fire	brothers
parents	trees	trains	feelings	

● List these under the following headings:

Things/people	Emotions
Trains	Hate

● Now you have to get your thoughts ordered. Get in a group of three or four. Choose a subject from the Things/people list and brainstorm it as in the example.

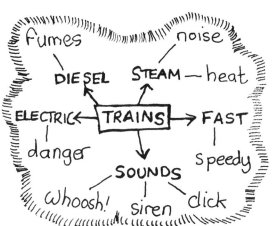

● Do the same for a subject on the other list.
● Which did you find it easier to brainstorm? Things/people or emotions? Why?
● Knowing which one you find easiest might help you to make a decision about your entry for the competition. Now write 100 words in sentences about your subject. Easy or difficult? Choose another and do the same thing again.

● I have decided that the subject (not title) of my entry to the *Schools' Poetry Association* competition is...
● I chose this because...

FORMATIONS

Once you have decided what you are going to write about, you need to decide how the poem is going to be written Below is a list of different forms of poems. See if you can write down something about each one. e.g. *Limerick.......a funny poem which.....etc*

BLANK VERSE

SHAPE POEM

RHYME

HAIKU

LIMERICK

A LIMERICK IS

A SHAPE POEM IS

A HAIKU IS

A RHYMING POEM IS

A BLANK VERSE POEM IS

Here are some examples of the types above.
● What form/type of poem is each one?
● Fill in the missing words from the poems using the word bank (remember that some poems have a pattern which you must follow).

WORD BANK
exits man moon shadows said honest slithery stood men carefully shaded says seven saying honestly slyly grinning London floor Londoner moonlight lino women
CHOOSE your words from the list.

Bright the full........shines;
On the matting of the floor,
...............of the pines.

All the world's a stage,
And all the men and ......
merely players:
They have their ..... and their entrances;
And one man in his time plays many parts,
His acts being .... ages

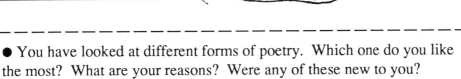

There was an old.......of Darjeeling,
Who travelled from.........to Ealing
It........on the door,
"Please don't spit on the..........."
So he spat on the ceiling.

Whoever treadeth on this stone
I pray you tread most neatly
For underneath this same do lie
Your.........friend, Will Wheatly

● You have looked at different forms of poetry. Which one do you like the most? What are your reasons? Were any of these new to you?
● You may have an idea of how to write your poem, but note that some forms of poetry are unsuitable for the subject.   e.g. would you write a sad, love poem in the form of a limerick?
● The subject of my poem is _____
● The form of my poem is _____
● The reason why I matched these two is_____

This page may be photocopied for classroom use only.

PEN TO PAPER

Now it's the time to start your poem. Follow these steps.

STEP 1 Choose your general subject. (Consider the world around you, things you feel strongly about, your memories).
My subject/s is/are..

STEP 2 Brainstorm ideas about this subject on your own. Use a large sheet of paper to write your ideas on.

STEP 3 Cut out all the indidual words and phrases. These are 'Building-bricks' of your poem to be made into the wall of your choice.

STEP 4 Arrange your words/phrases into patterns, shapes and combinations. When you find something that pleases you, copy it down onto a separate sheet. (you can add/take away words as you go along)

STEP 5 Now choose the form of the poem (its shape/sound). Are there any forms that would suit your poem (e.g. rhyme)?

WRITE YOUR FIRST COMPLETE VERSION OF THE POEM.

STOP ! WARNING!
Have you done any of the following:
● Used boring words *nice..lovely..really..very?*
● Repeated words unnecessarily?
● Used words ending in 'ing' too often which sound too much the same?
● Used words you are not really happy with?
THINK AGAIN.
● Produce a **second** draft, a **third** or as many as necessary! When you think you have finished your poems, swap with your friends.
1. What did your friend write about?
2. What did you like about the work?
3. What form did they use? Was it a good choice?
4. Were there any changes you would make?
5. What were their comments about yours?

● Now write your final, final version! Remember, this is an entry in a competition, so send it off. You can 'post' your entry to your teacher.

───

● I have completed my poem after a lot of hard work.
My title is...
(Choose a title carefully. It should be part of what you want your poem to say.)

YOU THE JUDGE

You have been selected to judge the *Schools' Poetry Association Poetry Competition*. You are very proud to have been chosen. The problem is, you've never done this before. How do you pick the winners? You can't just say "it was the best". All these are things you might look for in a poem. Put them in order of importance.

It was enjoyable.
It made you laugh.
It made you feel sad.
It made you think about something in a new way.
The words were interesting.
It painted a picture in your mind.
It told a good story.
It was original; you hadn't read one like this before.
The shape fitted the subject of the poem.
It sounded good when read aloud.
The start and end were good.
The title added to the understanding of the poem.

● Compare your findings with a friend
a. Write a whole class list in order.
b. Discuss where you disagreed and say why.
● Sue Townsend (author of *Adrian Mole*) said at the 1986 National Poetry Competition for children that originality was always the first thing that she looked for. Do you agree with her?

● Imagine this poem was one of the competition entries. Write-down your views about it, (BE HONEST) using the list above to help you. Which of these words can you use to describe poems?
Monotonous Stimulating Confusing Tedious Unclear Dull Surprising Original

The Washing Machine
It goes fwunkety
then shlunkety
as the washing goes around
The water splunches
and it sluncheses
as the washing goes around.
As you pick it out it splocheses,
then it flocheses,
as the washing goes around.
But at the end it schloppersies,
and then flopperies,
and the washing stops going
around.

● Once more discuss what you wrote with a friend. Did you agree?
● **RESULTS**
Choose the rank order, write the results down, and pass them to your teacher. He/she will then announce the overall winner.
● **WINNERS 'CORNER**
The winners can make a recording of their winning entries for the school records. An illustrated display of all the entries could be put up.

NEWS SPEAK

A new cable TV channel is to be launched. What is unique about this channel is that all the programmes are in *verse!* One programme which needs to be radically changed is the news.

PROGRAMME   The News
DETAILS
TIME
LENGTH
PRESENTERS
NUMBER OF ITEMS
SPECIAL FEATURES

STEP 1 RECRUIT YOUR TEAM.
You will need at least four people
STEP 2 GET YOUR NEWS.
Decide on the items for the programme (real or made-up news.......e.g. 'Dog swims Channel') Make a list of the reading order.
STEP 3 UP TO YOU, DIRECTOR!
Hand out the items to the team members.
STEP 4 VERSE VERSIONS.
The tricky bit! Put your reports into poetry like the examples below.

Item 1....Dog swims Channel...........

Item 2.....................................

Item 3.....................................

Item 4.....................................

Item 5.....................................

Item 6.....................................

Close......................................

Good evening to you,
Here is the news,
We hope we inform,
And don't give the blues.

● From which countries do these report-poems come? How would you use these in a news item? What are Michelle's feelings? Could you write your poems this way?

We do not see our neighbour's poverty
We do not hear hungry children cry
With outstretched arms
For a mother who can barely talk
And a father who is no more
Than a pile of bones
Laying unnoticed upon a dust road track.
And why, I say to myself
The greed for money?

From *'Shame on you!'* by **Michelle Kennedy.**

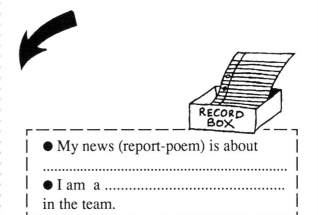

● My news (report-poem) is about

....
● I am a ....
in the team.

Time 5.00 pm
The Director calls you in to his office. He/she wants to hear your report. Each report is read out and timed exactly. The Director fills in the 'running order' sheet.

REHEARSAL
Time 5.30 pm. Have a first run through of intro, items and ending. Director times whole thing. Any changes needed?

Time 5.45 pm. Set up studio. Checklist: Scripts? Name-plates? Music?
(If you are recording then NOW is the time to set up your video camera or tape recorder)

Time 5.50 pm. FINAL run through.

Time 6.00 pm. TRANSMISSION TIME! You're on the air!

Time 6.30 pm. Finished! Phew! But, it's not all over yet. The director calls the team into the ofice again. In turn you are asked how you think the programme went. What did you enjoy? Which items worked best in verse? Any improvements you could make?

NEWS AT 6 O'CLOCK

PROGRAMME	TIME	LENGTH	TITLE
Introduction	6.00pm	10 seconds	Introduction
News item 1			
News item 2			
News item 3			

SUCCESS! The programme was so good, you've all been asked to join the team planning next week's schedules; not just news, either. What sort of programme do you think would be good in verse? Here are the football results....

You tell me

Here are the football results:
League division fun
Manchester United won,
Manchester City lost.
Crystal Palace 2, Buckingham Palace 1
Milwall Leeds nowhere
Wolves 8 A cheese roll and had a cup of tea 2
Aldershot 3, Buffalo Bill shot 2.
Everton nill, Liverpool's not very well either.
Newcastle 7, Sunderland's a very nice place 2.
Ipswich 1? You tell me.

Michael Rosen

- Can you think of any punning results yourself?
- What was the most difficult part of making the programme?

TALK RIGHT!

This is a rather strange poem. Nobody talks like this! Or do they? The poet is talking about a news programme that he's seen. Now read the poem to yourself aloud. Is it easier to understand?

right
i mean
me and me
mates ya know
was gleggin at
the telly the
uvver night
right
and well
i fort
most geezers wooten
believe
this bloke
and wot was
spoutin from
his norf and souf
if he spoke
like me
right
dolled up in
his wissel and floot
right
a posh voice
can only
tell the troof
right
in school
we was tort the
right
way to talk
right
this is my way
right
take it
or leave it
right

Dave Briggs

When we listen to the news most of us expect to hear STANDARD ENGLISH. What do you think standard English is? Is it just talking with a posh accent? Is this poem written in "Standard English"? What accent is it "written"in?

● Try to " translate" the poem. Here are the first few lines: *"My friends and I were watching the television the other night.."*
● The view of the poet, is that the audience wouldn't believe the news was true if it was read in an accent. What do you think of this view?
● Why do people have an accent? Do you think people with "posh" accents are more intelligent?
● Can you think how many people with accents are used in TV? For example, how many in situation comedies? Advertisements?
● Think of a strong accent you know. It might be your own. Try to write a poem (or a story if you prefer) which sounds like that accent when read out loud - like Dave's.

"yer what?"

"I say, my man, could you direct me to the town library please?"

● Find out what a STEREOTYPE is. People with accents often get STEREOTYPED just because of the way they speak. Do you think this is fair?

This page may be photocopied for classroom use only.

Poetry isn't just a modern invention. In the early days, poetry was a way of maintaining a story through generations by using the oral tradition. People would memorise poetry and recite it.

● A poem often rhymes and it is easier to remember. Which do you often find easier to remember, a pop song which rhymes, or a page from a novel? Can you explain why?
● How many different LANGUAGES can you name? You may even be skilled enough to speak more than one language yourself.

The English language has not always been the same as it is now and this can be seen if you look at poems which were written a long time ago
● Below is a section from a poem which was written in about the year 1285. It is called **'HAVELOK THE DANE'** and you can guess from the title what country the story came from (although the poet lived in England).

Te king was hoten Atelwold,
Of word, of wepne he was bold,
In Engeland was neure kniht,
Tat betere held te lond to riht.

You can imagine the scene when this story would be told. The king and all his men would be gathered together in a great hall one evening in order to swap stories of their bravery in battle and to hear similar stories recited by the *scop* or minstrel. This story is 3000 lines long!
As you read the poem you will recognise certain words which are the same today.

● Make a list of all the words which you can recognise.
● Here is a translation of some of the other words:
to riht = properly; *te* = the;
hoten = called; *wepne* = weapons;
neure = never; *lond* = country;
kniht = knight; *tat* = that;
betere = better; *held* = was loyal.
● Now write out the modern version.
● Imagine that you are going to continue the poem. Follow the rhyming pattern and write THREE more verses to continue the story.

RECORD BOX

● As these Old English poems were made to be listened to, you could recite your version to the rest of the class or make a recording of the class poems.
● Try to find out some more about the poetry of the oral tradition such as ballads.
● You could turn the poem into a play.

This page may be photocopied for classroom use only.

Now we'll travel forward to the fourteenth century. *Geoffrey Chaucer* wrote in a type of English known as **Middle English.** This extract comes from a series of stories which he wrote about Pilgrims travelling to Canterbury called *The Canterbury Tales.*

This Nicholas anon let fle a fart,
As greet as it had been a thonder-dent,
That with the strook he was almoost
yblent;
And he was ready with his iren hoot,
And Nicholas amydde the ers he
smoot.....

The Miller's Tale

● These clues might help you understand the poem:
leet fle = let fly
thonder-dent = clap of thunder
strook = blast
yblent = blinded
hoot = hot
amydde = in the middle of
ers = rear

As you can see from this section of the story, Chaucer had quite a sense of humour! Some of the words have not changed either!
● In your own words describe what is happening in this section of the poem.
● **SHAKESPEARE** was writing two hundred years later than Chaucer, but the language which he used still seems very 'old - fashioned' by today's standards. Here is a verse from one of his poems.

Upon her head a platted hive of straw,
Which fortified her visage from the sun,
Whereon the thought might think sometime it saw
The carcase of a beauty spent and done.
Time hath not scythed all that youth begun,
Nor youth all quit; but spite of heaven's fell rage,
Some beauty peep'd through lattice of sear'd age.

A Lover's Complaint'

● What words do you do not understand in Shakespeare's poem? Try to guess what they mean.
● Shakespeare wrote some effective descriptions in his poetry. He tried to make you create pictures in your mind. To do this he would often use a figure of speech known as a **METAPHOR.** A metaphor works like this: One thing is said to **BE** something else. This might sound strange, but how many times have you said: *'He's a real wet blanket!'* or *'She's a real little monkey!'*
● Invent your own metaphors and pictures for the following:
eg **AN OLD MAN......**.*A bent and leafless oak tree*
A YOUNG WOMAN. FALSE TEETH.
GRASS. A DOG. CATS.

● Is Chaucer's writing what you would expect from so long ago?
● Find out the names and stories of the other *'Canterbury Tales'*.
● How does a simile differ from a metaphor?

WORD INVADERS

Imagine a fantastic stew. It is always on the boil, and it has been cooking for thousands of years. It contains spices and herbs from all over the world, although the meat is old English. It tastes terrific, because things are always being added and taken out.

THIS STEW IS THE ENGLISH LANGUAGE.

Many different countries have added their own words (like spices) to our language, although you may not see them as foreign.

ALL the different countries below have given us words..

INDIA ITALY HOLLAND GERMANY SCANDINAVIA FRANCE GREECE ARABIA

Can you name any words we use from these countries?

CROSSWORD

Across 1. Trousers for riding (HINDI 7 letters)
2. Musical instrument with keyboard (ITALIAN 5)
3. Fast food (GERMAN 9)
4. Tasty Pickle (HINDI 7)
5. Eating place (FRENCH 4)
6. Temporary place to stay (FRENCH 5)
7. Place of performance (GREEK 7)
8. To thump (SCANDINAVIAN 3)
Down 1. Permanent picture (GREEK 10)
2. Long story (SCANDINAVIAN 4)
3. Beer-like drink (GERMAN 5)
4. Alone (ITALIAN 4)
5. Slum area (ITALIAN 6)
6. Book of maps (GREEK 5)

One language we have given many of our words to is American. Do you think this is a separate language from English? Here is an American rap. You need to translate it into English. Change the words which are in italics.

Restroom Rap.

I was crunching my *chips* the other day,
I was sitting on the *hood* of my chevrolet,
I polished my *fender* till it shone like new,
The mirror, the door, my large *trunk* too.

Out of the *restroom* a cool *chick* came,
She said "Hey *Buddy,* what's your name?
The *faucet's* broken, I need a hand,
Can you change a *diaper*? My baby's damp".

Took off my *tuxedo*, in I went,
Said, "Hey pretty mama, I'm heaven sent!
But that there job was too tough for me,
I 'll stick to *homicide* and robbery!

Bongo Lee and Eartha Closit.

● Perform this in pairs, dividing the rap as you wish . Does it work with the "translated" words too?
● Write your own rap. Check the rhyming pattern and where the emphasised words are. If you cannot think of a subject, here are some ideas: (a) a day at the seaside (b) your favourite TV programme (c) an argument at a disco.

CULTURE TALK

● **TIME** is an influence on the type of poetry that a poet writes. Perhaps an even stronger influence is the **PLACE** where a person is born.

● **WHERE** and **WHEN** were you born? Do you still live in the same place? Look at the map of the world here. How many of the shaded countries can you name? How many foreign countries have you visited?

● Often all that we know about a country is what we read in travel brochures or see on the TV. How would you describe the following countries?
INDIA, AUSTRALIA, SOUTH AFRICA, UNITED KINGDOM, WEST INDIES, NIGERIA. Which one would you like to live in and why?

● Match up the extracts from the poems below to the correct country and poet. There are clues in the poems. Look at the WORDS.

.......two old poets,
Hunched at their beer in the low haze
Of an inn parlour, while the talk ran
Noisily by them, glib with prose.

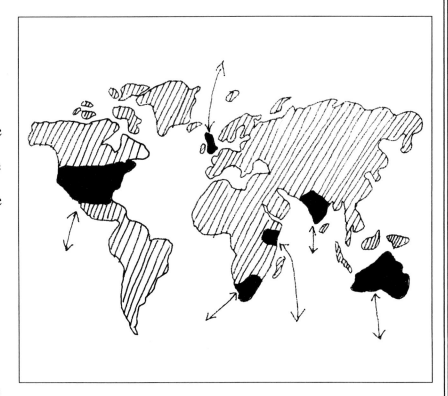

> **A.R. Cliff-Lubwa,**
> **EAST AFRICA**

......my old bones will lie
comforted with the elegance of
my white sari
and my elegant porcelain

> **H.D Carberry,**
> **WEST INDIES**

Lapobo,
Her teeth are not as ash
Nor the colour of maize flour,
Her teeth are white as fresh milk,
The whiteness of her teeth
When I think of her
Makes my food drop from my hand.
Lapobo,
Black but not too black,
Brown but not too brown,
Her skin colour is just between black and brown.

> **R.S. Thomas,**
> **UK**

We have neither summer nor winter,
Neither autumn nor spring.
We have instead the days
When the gold sun shines on the lush green canefields-
Magnificently.

> **Suniti Namjoshi,**
> **PAKISTAN**

● For each of the poems, say what words told you which country they came from.
● Imagine that you are going to write a poem which will reveal which part of the country you come from. What words would you use?
e,g. Pits, pottery, industry, railways might suit the Midlands.
● Try writing this short poem using your words.

● What do you dislike most about where you live?
● How would you recommend your area to someone about to move into it?

Poets from different countries often write about the people of their land. People within any country are very different, but we often have a view of the typical type of person who lives in a country, and this is known as a **STEREOTYPE.** In the UK we are often stereotyped as being upper-class, posh, horsey, tweed-wearing and old-fashioned! How true to life do you think this is?

● Here is a poem about a person. His nationality has been missed out. What country do you think he comes from?

I'm a fullblooded
********** *stereotype*
See me straw hat?
Watch it good
I'm a fullblooded
********** *stereotype*
You ask
if I got riddum
in me blood
You going to ask!
Man just beat de drum
and don't forget
to pour de rum

● What made you reach your decision? Do you think that this was a fair choice to make?
Now read the final verse of the poem.

Yes I'm a fullblooded
West Indian stereotype
that's why I
graduated from Oxford
University
with a degree
in anthropology.

John Agard.

● What do you think of the poet now?
● In your own words, write what you think he is saying in the poem.

● What are the usual stereo-types for the following nationalities?
RUSSIAN, AMERICAN, MEXICAN, AUSTRALIAN.
Now, for each one, write what you really know about the people.

● Here are some poems written about people from different countries.

Beggar

Shadowed
by the minaret,
she stoops
to gather scraps -
shrivelled pieces -
dessicated food.
Her withered hands,
joints like
gnarled tree-roots,
scratch pathetically
at dried earth
or
are held out -
entreating.

Tariq Hussain

Old Ladies Home

Sharded in black, like beetles,
Frail as antique earthenware
One breath might shiver to bits,
The old women creep out here
To sit on the rocks or prop
Themselves up against the wall
Whose stones keep a little heat

Sylvia Plath

● These poems are both about old people. Which one is from Pakistan? How do you know?
● How are the lives of the two old people different?

RECORD BOX

┌ ─ ─ ─ ─ ─ ─ ─ ─ ┐
| ● Write a poem about an old |
| person who you know. It |
| could be a relative or just |
| someone who you have seen. |
| Think of the way that they |
| move and talk. Where do |
| they live? What do they do? |
| ● It would be good to match |
| your poem up to a photo- |
| graph or picture. |
└ ─ ─ ─ ─ ─ ─ ─ ─ ┘

● Poetry has often been used by people to put across their strongest feelings - love, hate, regret, and particularly anger. Have you ever written about something which makes you angry?

Shame on you!
Money makes the world go round they say.
Ha, I reply.
For I know that this world which once revolved on love,
Is slowly coming to a halt.
And why?
Money.

● Michelle Kennedy is clearly angry. What is she angry about?

● Make a list of the things which make you feel angry.

● As a class, make a list of the things which make most of you angry.

● A lot of poeple are made angry because of the place that they live. Can you think of any of the examples of people like this?

Here is a poem written by Mbuyiseni Oswald Mtshali who lives in South Africa.

KEEP OFF THE GRASS

The grass is a green mat
trimmed with gladioli
red like flames in a furnace.
The park bench, hallowed,
holds the loiter listening
to the chant of the fountain
showering holy water on a congregation
of pigeons.

KEEP OFF THE GRASS
DOGS NOT UNDER LEASH FORBIDDEN.

Then madam walks her Pekinese,
bathed and powered and perfumed.
He sniffs at the face of the 'Keep Off' sign
with a nose as cold as a frozen fish
and salutes it with a hind paw
leaving it weeping in anger and shame.

● How does the poet feel about the woman and her dog? Why does he call her 'MADAM'?
● Who is the 'Keep off' sign really for?
● What do you feel about the place where this man lives?

● Work with a group of four . Make a list of all the things about our society which you dislike or which make you angry.

● You are going to write a group poem. The first words of each line of the poem will be.........*It's not fair*.........You can put all the ideas of the group into the poem.
eg. *It's not fair that we breathe in smog and lead,*
Its not fair.........
The last line of your poem should be *It's not fair!*

● You can try recording or videoing your group's poem or you could make up a display with pictures to go with the lines of the poem.
● Rather than end on a sad note, you and your group could write another poem with each line beginning *It's great*........

DOCUMENT DECISION

As the senior researcher for *Channel Four* you have been given a very important job, to make a film about Shakespeare and his poetry. Your film will be one of a series of documentaries called **POETRY PEOPLE.**

● You have to put together some information about Shakespeare's life. Not much is known about this, but your junior researcher has really become **CONFUSED!** You have to sort out the true statements from the false ones in the list below.

Shakespeare was born in the 16th Century.
He was the son of a photographer.
He was born in Glasgow.
He wrote "The Merchant of Venice".
He rode to work in Milton Keynes on his bicycle.
He married Anne Hathaway.
He wrote "Macbeth".
He visited America twice.
He died in 1616.
Henry VIII was King for most of Shakespeare's life.
He wrote "The Importance of Being Earnest".
His plays were often performed at the Palladium theatre.

● There are only five true statements. Try to find out the true statement for each of the incorrect ones.

● Just to make your job more difficult, the producer has decided that you should present the introduction to the programme in the form of a poem, to be filmed in four different locations. You have to write FOUR verses based around the following ideas. It is left up to you whether you decide to rhyme the poem or not.

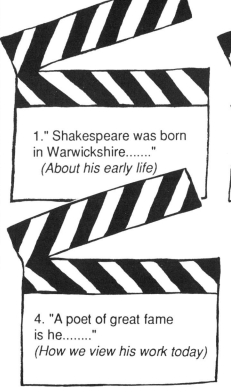

1." Shakespeare was born in Warwickshire......."
 (About his early life)

2. "A clever lad,
 to London he went........."
 (About his early years as a writer)

3. "Fair Queen Bess
 adored his plays......."
 (He becomes famous.)

4. "A poet of great fame is he........"
 (How we view his work today)

● For each of the verses you have to decide on a LOCATION where that section will be filmed. Try to be imaginative - don't just film everything in Stratford-Upon-Avon!

This page may be photocopied for classroom use only.

Here is a very famous **sonnet** which was written by William Shakespeare.

Shall I compare thee to a summer's day?
Thou art more lovely and more temperate.
Rough winds do shake the darling buds of May,
And summer's lease hath all too short a date:
Sometimes too hot the eye of heaven shines,
And often is his gold complexion dimm'd
And every fair from fair some time declines,
By chance, or nature's changing course, untrimm'd;
But thy eternal summer shall not fade
Nor lose possession of that fair thou ow'st;
Nor shall death brag thou wand'rest in his shade,
When in eternal lines to time thou grow'st.
So long as men can breathe or eyes can see,
So long lives this, and this gives life to thee.

The **SONNET** is a very rigid form pattern. It has 14 lines and a very set rhyme scheme.

● In the table below, put together the pairs of words which rhyme in the order that they appear in the poem.

DAY					
MAY					

● What is different about the rhyming pattern of the last **TWO** lines? This is known as a **RHYMING COUPLET.** It finishes off a verse or a poem in a very neat way.
● What is Shakespeare saying in this couplet? **CLUE:** What is *lovely* about summer?
● Now try writing your own alternative rhyming couplet as an ending to the sonnet. (You may also have noticed that each line has **TEN** syllables, so you have to follow the same pattern.)
Here are some ways of starting off-
'If I could ....' or *' My life with you ....'*
● A tricky job! You have to put the sonnet into a film format (a bit like making a pop video).
Use the story board to plan your film. Use one box for the title and each other box for two lines each. You could either make up a story or use a lot of different images. Write down your ideas first and sort them out.

RECORD BOX

● I made a film about.....................
....
....
● I chose this because....................
....
....
....

DISCOVERED!

During you research into Shakespeare`s life, you discover something totally new - he was very closely involved with the **SPANISH ARMADA,** writing about it for Queen Elizabeth! In the dusty attic of an old Elizabethan manor-house, you discover an amazing document! A signed sonnet from Shakespeare to Queen Elizabeth all about the Armada!

What a find!

BUT

You tell everybody!

The sonnet goes missing and you need it for the filming tomorrow!

DISASTER!

Fame at last!

LUCKILY you have not shown it to anyone. So you hatch the plan to rewrite it yourself.

FIRST: Make sure that you have the correct information. Study the copy of the original historical document here. **ALSO** bear in mind that Queen Elizabeth liked to be flattered. If Shakespeare wanted to keep his head it would have been a good idea to say some flattering things about his monarch!

We whose names are her under written have determyned and agreed in councaile to folowe and pursue the Spanishe Fleete untill we have cleared oure owne coaste and broughte the Firthe weste of us and then to returne backe againe as well to revictuall oure ships whiche stande in estrem scarsitie and also to guard and defend oure owne coaste at home with further protestatione that if oure wants of victualles and munitione were suppliede we wold pursue them to the furthest that they durste have gone.

Charles Lord Howard of Effingham   Francis Drake
George Earl of Cumberland   Edward Hoby
Lord Thomas Howard   John Hawkins
Edmund Lord Sheffield   Thomas Fenner

1 Augusti 1588

SECOND: Make sure that your sonnet is set out properly. Fill in the spaces below:
● A sonnet has .... lines
● The rhyming pattern is ....
● Each line has .... syllables.
● The poem ends in a rhyming couplet like this ....

THIRD : You need to try to copy the Elizabethan vocabulary. What words would be out? *Computer? Telephone? Gorgeous? Photograph? Submarine? Missile? Radar?* Start to write your replacement sonnet. Draft it out as many times as you need to before you write it up finally. When you are satisfied, write out your sonnet authentically.

THE FINAL TEST: Perform your *'NEWLY DISCOVERED SONNET'* in front of a film camera

CRITICAL REACTION: A lot of people have things to say. Swap your sonnet with that of a friend. What do you think? You might like to write your views as if they were an article in a newspaper.

COVER-UP

Here are some covers of poetry anthologies. What do you think each collection is about judging from the covers? War? Trains?

The idea you have decided upon could be what all the poems in the anthology have in common and is called the **theme.**

A THEME is also the important idea that runs through a poem. Many poems have more than one. Themes might be ...... *loneliness, fear, joy, birth, racism, childhood, travel etc.* Which of these is the theme and title of the poem below?

● Write a collection of the poems on one of the themes above and design your own cover for the anthology.

● In a group, chose a new theme together. Now see if you can find poems on that theme. Where would you go? Next, decide which ones are to be included, and how you are going to arrange them in your anthology (by author? by title?)

● Imagine you are a publisher. You receive hundreds of ideas for poetry collections. Here are some of their titles. You can't read them all, so which would you choose from their titles? What do you think each is about?

Making Cocoa for Kingsley Amis.
Breasting the Tide.
Moortown.
The Rattle Bag.
Speaking to You.
Up the line to Death.

They are all real collections, you may have come across the more well-known ones.

I rode the waves,
on a surf-board of silence

I flew round the world,
In a leopard moth of flies.

I skied down the mountain,
On skies of slowness.

I soared the sky,
On a hang-glider of height.

I sailed the sea
In a boat of barnacles.

Nicholas Robus (10)

● Underline all the verbs of movement in the poem.

LOVE STORY

A common theme in poetry is relationships, particularly where love is concerned. Look at the way Elvis Costello deals with it in the extract from his song *Everyday I write a book*. He uses the image of a book to help us understand the "story" of his love.

Chapter One, we didn't really get along,
Chapter Two, I think I fell in love with you.
You said you'd stand by me in the middle of chapter three,
But you were up to your old tricks in chapters four, five and six.

And everyday I write a book...

Don't tell me you don't know the difference,
Between a lover and a fighter,
With my pen and electric typwriter,
Even in a perfect world where everyone was equal,
I'd still own the film rights and be working on the sequel.

● Using such an image more than once to explain more clearly the point of your poem, or to paint a picture in the reader's mind, is called an **EXTENDED METAPHOR** - you *extend* its use. This describes something as if it was something else completely! List the words connected with "story" that Elvis Costello has used in his song.

HAPPY ENDINGS.
● Write the story behind this poem. Give two alternative endings, one happy, one sad. Which works best?
● Imagine a peaceful, stable , calm relationship. Which of the things below would fit in a poem about such a friendship?
a boat on a pond: a rocky climb :
a rollercoaster : a walk through mud.

In another song Elvis Costello says *You were the spice of life, the gin in my vermouth.* Does he mean she was a herb in the kitchen? Of course not! Explain the metaphor.

● Match up the most suitable metaphors with the real life issues below.

Real life issues.	Metaphors.
Hunger	a flower bud
Divorce	an icicle on a hot day
Fear	a child's broken toy
Youth	a withered tree

● My favourite metaphor on this sheet was..
● I liked it because ....
● Where does the word METAPHOR come from? What does it mean LITERALLY? You will have to split the word into two parts.

HIDDEN TALENTS

We all have secret interests and talents even our friends don't know about. Poems are like this too .... they have hidden surprises, unusual ideas, and use subtle skills. This poem is about the Wild West, but you may need to do a little research to find out who Mr Earp was.

Tombstone Library

In Tombstone there was, it seems
a public library
between the marshall's office
and the Silver Lode Saloon
On endless, silent afternoons
the clicking of the faro wheel
the tired piano's nervous twinkle
scratching the library's wooden walls
I like to think of them
the whores and gamblers
the faro dealers and the mining men
cool in the library's silent shade
whispering their silent way through 'Romance'
and 'Ancient History'
soft spurs jingling past the rows of books
the half-breed coughing gently over 'War and Peace'
And at the issue desk
a stocky figure in a bowler hat
'I'm sorry Mr Earp, this book is overdue'
He bends and fumbles
flicks out a coin and smiles
(his teeth are not yet film-star white)
dark and nervous as a cat
He turns and moves towards 'Mythology'.

Richard Hill

How can we find words to write or say about why and how this poem works? Well, there are several ways.

● With a friend, discuss any lines/phrases/ words that stand out, or that you like. Can you say why you noticed them?
● Try to describe as simply as possible what the story of the poem is (eg. some cowboys visit the library?)
● Choose the line that you find most difficult in the poem and interrogate it (ask it questions) .... *what does this word mean? I don't know; do I know words like it?* etc.
● Make some lists under these headings :

SOUNDS	IMAGES (pictures)
jingling	a stocky figure

● Try to write a hundred words on the atmosphere of the poem. Is it exciting? Quiet? Funny?
● What is the *hidden side* that Mr Earp shows?
● Why is it **ironic** that he should be looking for books in 'Mythology'? Check in the glossary.

This page may be photocopied for classroom use only.

MIND WORDS

It is clear that good poets choose their words carefully. Your teacher probably spends a lot of time making sure you don't use boring words, or repeat yourself too often..... just like the teacher in this poem.

TEACHER SAID...

You can use
mumbled and muttered,
groaned, grumbled and uttered,
professed, droned or stuttered
.....but *don't* use **SAID.**

You can use
rant or recite,
yell, yodel or snort,
bellow murmur or moan,
you can grunt or just groan
.....but *don't* use **SAID.**

You can
hum, howl and hail,
scream, screech, shriek or bawl,
squeak, snivel or squeal
with a blood-curdling wail
.....but *don't* use **SAID.**

Judith Nicholls

● Read the poem to yourself and decide what the alternatives to *say* mean (eg. *scream = cry out in a high pitched voice*). If you don't know, look them up in a dictionary.

● Read the poem aloud with a friend, dividing the poem as you wish. Say each word in the way it is described (eg. scream *'Scream'!*) This will make for a noisy, but enjoyable time!

● These alternatives are all **verbs.** They say what someone is doing: *'you howl'*, *'she yells'* etc. Can any of these be turned into adjectives? e.g. *squeak* becomes *squeaky*.

● Write a story that includes all these verbs. You may convert them to adjectives where necessary. Does it make it easier or more difficult?

| ● **VERBS** are magic spells. They make things come to life. Here is a still picture in words, mainly nouns:

blue/white sky   cotton-wool clouds   small sun
distant boat   smoke on horizon   waves
girl on beach   sleepy dog   sandcastles

EVERYTHING is frozen by the spell. Cast your own spell by adding verbs to this scene, so that the cotton-wool clouds *drift* in the breeze...and so on. Make this into a poem. Remember what 'teacher said'!

      This page may be photocopied for classroom use only.

PRESS FOR ACTION

You are the new editor of a poetry magazine. Your first job is to decide what is going to be included in it. The previous editor left some suggestions .... but some don't seem to fit.

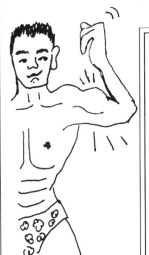

1. An interview with Arnold Schwarzenneger
2. Some new poems by Russian children
3. The latest rugby results
4. An account of a visit to Anne Hathaway`s cottage
5. An extract from a play called '*Under Milk Wood*'
6. An interview with Ted Hughes
7. A recipe for syllabub
8. An article about the use of syllables
9. An article on epitaphs and gravestones
10. An interview with Imran Khan
11. An article about Habib Jalib

● Which do you think could be included? You may need to do some research. Here is one of the gravestones. Why should this be included?

In Memory of
Benjamin Linton
blacksmith
who ˌed Oct 10 1842 aged 80

His sledge and hammer
lie reclined
His bellows too have
lost their wind
His fire extinct
his forge decayed
His vice all in the dust
Is laid
His coal is spent
his iron gone
His last nail's driven
his work is done

● What connections with poetry does this have? You decide this is worth including. Can you find any others? This might mean a trip to the local cemetery.

● Write an account of your visit, either real or fictional. Try to convey what it is like to visit such a sad place.

● If you can face it, write your own epitaph. It should include some reference to the type of person you are, what you liked/disliked etc.

● Find out the names of any poetry magazines. Write down which title you like best and why you like it.

FRONT PAGE

Here are some articles from the front page of your magazine. Unfortunately, they're rather muddled, as someone has dropped them and in some cases pieces are incomplete. Sort them out and finish them where necessary. Research may be needed.

TRIBUTE TO POET LAUREATE
INFO INSIDE
AGONY AUNT POEM
THREE POEMS IN A MINUTE
SONNETS DISCOVERED
NEW SHAKESPEARE LOVE

Stunning news hit the literary wor
English, Edith Ethelbert, found orig
She had been sifting through the
cottage when she came across the p
....delighted and........by th

Problem Page

Dear Claire,
I am a young sapling,
and at six minutes to six
every evening precisely,
a thin, scruffy canine
attempts liquid communication.
When he arrives,
he sniffs my trunk encouragingly,
moves his small and hairy rear
and then lifts his leg.
What can I do
to convince him
that I am not thirsty?
Confused
Betty Rootanbranch.

Today, we remember the Queen's
poet who died almost.....years
ago, aged .....Sir John was born
in ....and educated at.......
Two of his most famous poems were
"Hunter ......" and "A Subaltern's Love Song"
with its immortal line: "Miss J Hunter Dunn,
Miss J Hunter Dunn,
Furnished and burnished by...........sun"

ld this morning. A senior professor of
inal manuscripts dating back to....
papers in the attic at Ann Hathaway's
archment in a trunk. She said that she
e find. Special report centre page....

ate a limerick,a sonnet and a
erday, instead of reading . His
.......by his actions. "He's never
ys said sausages were his favourite."
below....We asked him why he did it.
..."

RECORD BOX

A schoolboy, Jasper Mudd aged 11
villanelle at the school concert yest
mother was said to be........and.....
done nothing like this before, he alwa
An interview with Jasper is included
He said.... "Well my mate Curtis........

Have you ....
● Completed the articles? Try writing about 100 words for each one.
● Designed your page?
● Found the poems mentioned?
● You could write your own problem page poem like the one printed above.

POETIC POWER

Halib Jalib is a poet from Pakistan. He writes "political" poetry about things which he considers very important. Where do we find political writing in this country?

On the banning of a book of poems.

In my hand I hold a pen
in my heart the light of consciousness.
How can your forces of oppression
ever win?
I, concerned with peace for all mankind
and you just out to save your precious skin.
Into the world I dawn, the rising sun;
Into the ocean of oblivion you shall sink!

● In Box **A** are some words that are often associated with writing that is making a point. Match up the words in Box **A** with the definitions in Box **B**, then the examples in Box **C**.

A
BIAS   OPINION
REASON

B
A one-sided view of events
A considered, thoughtful attitude
A belief

C
Stephen Hendry is the greatest snooker player.
If you drive too fast you are likely to have an accident.
All the evidence (we asked many Scots) shows that the British want Scotland to have its independence.

In some countries, poetry is still a good, but dangerous way, of saying what you feel.

My daughter.

Thinking it was a toy,
when she saw the chain around
my wrists
my daughter jumped for joy.

Her laughter was the gift of morning,
her laughter gave me endless strength.
A living hint of a free tomorrow
gave meaning to my night of sorrow.

● There are some difficult words in the poem *On the Banning of a Book of Poems*. eg. "oppression" and "oblivion". Find out what they mean. Why might a book of poetry be banned? Who would ban it?
● If the poet is like "the rising sun" what does that tell us about his hopes? What does he think will happen to his enemies?
● Chidren are said not to see evil in the world. How is this shown in *My Daughter* ?

● Find more poetry from India, Pakistan and Bangladesh. See if you can find poetry by Kishwar Naheed, Zulfikar Ghose, Rabindrath Tagore or Habib Jalib. Investigate the work and ideas of one of these poets.

POETIC POWER

Halib Jalib is a poet from Pakistan. He writes "political" poetry about things which he considers very important. Where do we find political writing in this country?

On the banning of a book of poems.

In my hand I hold a pen
in my heart the light of consciousness.
How can your forces of oppression
ever win?
I, concerned with peace for all mankind
and you just out to save your precious skin.
Into the world I dawn, the rising sun;
Into the ocean of oblivion you shall sink!

● In Box **A** are some words that are often associated with writing that is making a point. Match up the words in Box **A** with the definitions in Box **B**, then the examples in Box **C**.

In some countries, poetry is still a good, but dangerous way, of saying what you feel.

My daughter.

Thinking it was a toy,
when she saw the chain around
my wrists
my daughter jumped for joy.

Her laughter was the gift of morning,
her laughter gave me endless strength.
A living hint of a free tomorrow
gave meaning to my night of sorrow.

A

BIAS   OPINION
REASON

B

A one-sided view of events
A considered, thoughtful attitude
A belief

C

Stephen Hendry is the greatest snooker player.
If you drive too fast you are likely to have an accident.
All the evidence (we asked many Scots) shows that the British want Scotland to have its independence.

● There are some difficult words in the poem *On the Banning of a Book of Poems*. eg. "oppression" and "oblivion". Find out what they mean. Why might a book of poetry be banned? Who would ban it?
● If the poet is like "the rising sun" what does that tell us about his hopes? What does he think will happen to his enemies?
● Chidren are said not to see evil in the world. How is this shown in *My Daughter ?*

RECORD BOX

● Find more poetry from India, Pakistan and Bangladesh. See if you can find poetry by Kishwar Naheed, Zulfikar Ghose, Rabindrath Tagore or Habib Jalib. Investigate the work and ideas of one of these poets.

VISIONS

Poetry about Gods, goddesses and religion has always existed. But why do people want to write about ideas and people you cannot see? Well, perhaps you believe in visions. You're not the only one.

God throws the Devil down into hell in *Paradise Lost* by John Milton. This is what Satan sees....

The dismal situation waste and wild;
A dungeon horrible, on all sides round,
As one great furnace, flamed, yet from those flames
No light, but rather darkness visible
Served only to discover sights of woe,
Regions of sorrow, doleful shades, where peace
And rest can never dwell, hope never comes
That comes to all, but torture without end
Still urges, and a fiery deluge, fed
With ever-burning sulphur.......

● What is the story told in *Paradise Lost*?
● How is Hell described in the extract?
● Do you believe in heaven or Hell?
Describe your idea of one or both.

Pete Townsend's vision is more modern.

And I moved.

And I moved
As I saw him looking through my window
His eyes were silent lies
And I moved
And I saw him standing in the doorway
His figure merely filled the space
And I moved
But I moved toward him.

And I moved
And his hands felt like ice - exciting
As he laid me back just like an empty dress
And I moved
But a minute after he was weeping
His tears his only truth
And I moved
But I moved towards him.

● Who is *he*?
● Does *silent lies* tell us anything about Pete Townsend's initial reaction to the vision?
● What phrases suggest that the figure has power over Pete?
● What does *moved* mean in this instance?
● Write about your religious beliefs - or lack of them. You could write about a vision, real or imagined, in poetic form.

● *darkness visible* is an example of oxymoron, or a kind of paradox as used in *Paradise Lost*. What is meant by this?

RECORD BOX

This page may be photocopied for classroom use only.

VISIONS

Poetry about Gods, goddesses and religion has always existed. But why do people want to write about ideas and people you cannot see? Well, perhaps you believe in visions. You're not the only one.

God throws the Devil down into hell in *Paradise Lost* by John Milton. This is what Satan sees....

The dismal situation waste and wild;
A dungeon horrible, on all sides round,
As one great furnace, flamed, yet from those flames
No light, but rather darkness visible
Served only to discover sights of woe,
Regions of sorrow, doleful shades, where peace
And rest can never dwell, hope never comes
That comes to all, but torture without end
Still urges, and a fiery deluge, fed
With ever-burning sulphur.......

● What is the story told in *Paradise Lost*?
● How is Hell described in the extract?
● Do you believe in heaven or Hell?
Describe your idea of one or both.

Pete Townsend's vision is more modern.

And I moved.

And I moved
As I saw him looking through my window
His eyes were silent lies
And I moved
And I saw him standing in the doorway
His figure merely filled the space
And I moved
But I moved toward him.

And I moved
And his hands felt like ice - exciting
As he laid me back just like an empty dress
And I moved
But a minute after he was weeping
His tears his only truth
And I moved
But I moved towards him.

● Who is *he*?
● Does *silent lies* tell us anything about Pete Townsend's initial reaction to the vision?
● What phrases suggest that the figure has power over Pete?
● What does *moved* mean in this instance?
● Write about your religious beliefs - or lack of them. You could write about a vision, real or imagined, in poetic form.

● *darkness visible* is an example of oxymoron, or a kind of paradox as used in *Paradise Lost*. What is meant by this?

RECORD BOX

This page may be photocopied for classroom use only.

POETRY PRODUCT

YOUR OWN POETRY MAGAZINE

Below are the stages you might go through to create your own school poetry magazine.

CHOOSE YOUR EDITORIAL TEAM

These are the people who decide what to write about and know how and where to find subject matter. You will need someone in charge of layout, illustrations/photos, and promotion (making sure people buy/read it). You need to decide who the writers will be.

CHOOSE WHAT IS GOING IN IT

Are you going to include articles about poets, countries, different types of poems, poems by you, poems by friends, quizzes about poetry?

COLLECT MATERIAL

After you have collected your poems and articles you may like to hold a competition to encourage contributors.

PRESENTATION

You must decide how you are going to present your work - Hand-written? Typed?

EDIT

Select any articles/poems/illustrations you don't want, but make sure you consult your editorial team first. Who will make the final decision if you don't agree? Does anything need to be corrected?

PASTE UP

Once your articles are written you need to arrange them on the page. This will be the responsibility of the layout member of your team, but you can all help. Make sure you proof read all the poems and articles before and after paste-up to eliminate mistakes in spelling/copying up. If you have access to a word-processor/computer, then use it.

COVER AND TITLE

Once your pages are completed along with photos and pictures, add these things: a contents page, an introduction presenting the writers/editorial team, an index too (contents at the back). Now get your artist/designer to produce a cover. Make sure you have agreed on what you want first. Choose a title. Here are some real poetry magazine titles: *'Argo', 'Footnotes', 'Strength Beyond Bingo',* and *'Slow Dancer'*. Make sure your title fits what's inside!

OFFICIAL PRESENTATION

Invite people to the launch of the magazine. Where will it be held? In the school library? A class-room? At a friend's house? Who will you invite? A famous poet? The Head? Perhaps a favourite teacher?

ROOM FOR POETRY

Most of the work you have completed about poetry suggests that displaying it in some way would be a good idea. But how?

1. What do you want to display?
2. Do you need illustrations or drawings with it?
3. Are there things you want to display in the same way? Will you need different areas\headings ?

LOOKING GOOD.
How can you make your display look good?

Choose which of the following you think important for display.

COLOUR   TYPESCRIPT   PICTURES   THREE-DIMENSIONAL   WORK
ON THE WALL   ON THE CEILING   HANDWRITTEN   IN PENCIL
IN FELT TIP   BIRO   IN PAINT   CRAYON   USING PHOTOS
PHOTOS FROM....   TYPE AND COLOUR OF PAPER USED   CARD?

● How should poems look?
● How would you present the poem below on a sheet of A4 plain paper?

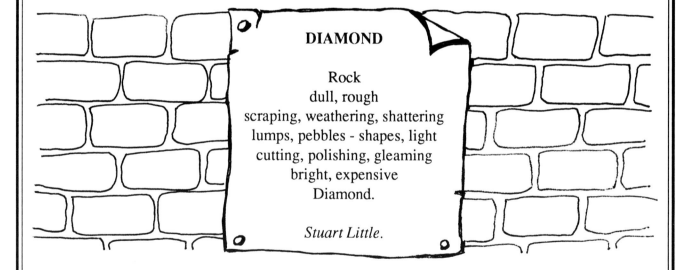

DIAMOND

Rock
dull, rough
scraping, weathering, shattering
lumps, pebbles - shapes, light
cutting, polishing, gleaming
bright, expensive
Diamond.

Stuart Little.

● You need to consider: what it is about, shape, length, size, position on the page, typed or hand-written?
● Now create your own display.

● REMEMBER...the display must draw attention to the poems. Who is the display for? How long will the work be on display? Will you send invitations to people who might want to see it?

POETRY PROFILE

Whether or not you have completed all the work in this course, it is always useful to look back at what you have done. Fill in the following to help you assess your awareness of poetry.

Name.   Class.   Teacher.

What is the earliest poem you remember from childhood? (A nursery rhyme? A song?)

Name three poets you can remember.

What is your favourite poem studied so far in this course? What did you like about it? What type of poem was it?

Write the titles of any poems you have written.

Which was your favourite and why? How many verses did it have? Did it rhyme? Your favourite lines and why?

RECORD BOX

● Which of the following do you remember studying?

Shakespeare, Cinquain, Conversation poems, Old English, Covers, Sonnets, Syllables, Raps, Epitaphs, Radio poetry, Competitions, Standard English, Stereotypes, Poetry from Pakistan, Haiku, Scripts, Themes.

● Write 50-100 words about the kind of activities which took place in these studies, and what you found out about at least one of the above.

● Now that you have developed your poetry-reading and writing skills and know a little more about the different types of poems and poets, it is time you tried to produce a final group of poems.
Write and collect together a group of poems on one of the following:
Childhood; My school life so far; My favourite things.

GLOSSARY

Abbreviation
Words shortened, eg. BBC, *dept.* for department.
Accent
Voice change because of region or country or a syllable that is emphasised or stressed.
Anthology
Collection of stories, poems etc, by theme eg. love, or genre, eg. limerick etc.
Article
Piece of writing in magazine/paper.
Brainstorm
Getting ideas by thinking of any words/phrases connected to the subject you are writing about.
Contents
List of parts of a book at front.
Culture
Group of people/society.
Editor
Person who decides contents of paper, programme, magazine etc.
Epitaph
Writing chosen for gravestone/tomb.
Fiction
Imaginative story/tale.
Form
Shape/layout of poem.
Headline
Main heading at top of front page of newspaper.
Index
List at back of book of people/things included.
Irony
Saying the opposite of what is meant; also, slight absurdity; (see *Hidden Talents* - Wyatt Earp's interest in 'Mythology' is ironic because he himself is a 'myth').
Phrase
Group of words that make sense together (not always full sentence).
Producer
Person responsible for organisation or final performance of play, programme, film etc.
Pun
A play/joke on the two meanings of a word/sound.
Proof-read
Check piece of writing for mistakes before final version.
Recite
Perform piece of writing (poem/part of play/speech) aloud.
Researcher
Person who finds out information about topic.
Re-draft
Re-write something altering it where necessary.
Script
A piece of drama or programme written down.
Sequence
Order of things/words.
Storyboard
Story told in drawings as preparation for tv/film broadcast.
Summary
Short version of story to include essential parts only.
Survey
Examination of people's habits/thoughts about something.
Transmission
Broadcast of programme on tv/radio.
Translation
Putting a piece of writing or what someone says from one language into another.
Verse
Part of a poem (often rhyming), that is separated from next part by a line or more.

YOUR REFERENCE

Sheet 8 - SOUNDS GOOD
The missing words are *mud* and *boots*.
The poem is entitled *Muddy Boots*.

Sheet 11 - SNAPSHOTS
The haiku originally read:
The cuckoo's note hangs
Sweetly in the still June trees
Fruit to be devoured.

Sheet 29 - WORD INVADERS
Across 1. Jodhpurs
2. Piano
3. Hamburger
4. Chutney
5. Cafe
6. Hotel
7. Theatre
8. Hit
Down 1. Photograph
2. Saga
3. Lager
4. Solo
5. Ghetto
6. Atlas

Sheet 41 - FRONT PAGE
Sir John Betjeman, Poet Laureate - born 1906, died 1985 - educated at Marlborough Public School.
The poem mentioned is entitled *Hunter Trials* and the missing word from *A Subaltern's Love Song* is "Aldershot".

USEFUL ADDRESSES

The Schools' Poetry Association
27 Pennington Close
Colden Common
Winchester SO21 1UR
Tel: 0962 712062

The Poetry Society
21 Earls Court Square
London SW5 9DE
Tel: 01 373 7861

The Poetry Library
The South Bank Centre
South Bank Board
Royal Festival Hall
London SE1 8XX
Tel:01 921 0943

Sheet 30 - CULTURE TALK
Here is the full text of two of the poems quoted.

The Little Chapel

When I am old and rich and gracious,
I shall have a little chapel in my garden,
And every morning I shall walk there,
Checking red roses and white.
I shall always pray in a white sari -
White is so becoming to prayer.
In the mornings I shall pray,
In the evenings pour tea.
And all the gracious ladies in the city
Will envy my tea ceremony.
And my old bones will lie comforted
With the elegance of my white sari
And my elegant porcelain.

Suniti Namjoshi, Pakistan

Nature

We have neither Summer nor Winter,
Neither Autumn nor Spring.

We have instead the days
When gold sun shines on the lush green canefields -
Magnificently.

The days when the rain beats like bullets on the roofs
And there is no sound but the swish of water in the gullies
And trees struggling in the high Jamaica winds.

Also there are the days when the leaves fade from off the guango trees
And the reaped canefields lie bare and fallow in the sun.

But best of all there are the days when the mango and the logwood blossom.

When the bushes are full of the sound of bees and the scent of honey,
When the tall grass sways and shivers to the slightest breath of air,
When the buttercups have paved the earth with yellow stars,
And beauty comes suddenly and the rains have gone.

H.D. Carberry, West Indies